Contents

Villains

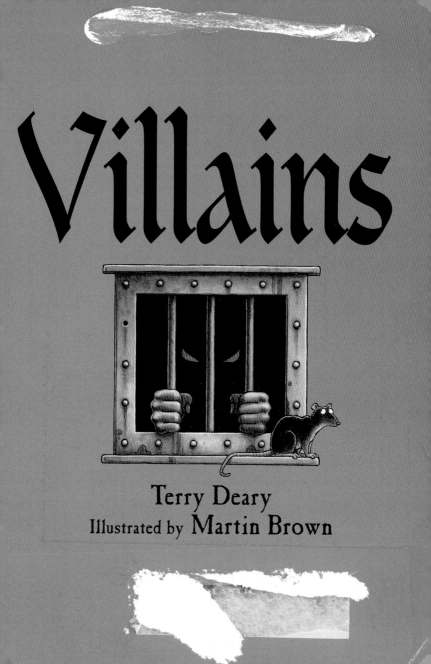

Terry Deary

Illustrated by Martin Brown

For Sara – the best one-legged researcher in the business. TD

To everyone who has worked on Horrible Histories,
past and present. MB

Editorial Director: Lisa Edwards
Editor: Victoria Garrard
Art Director: Richard Smith

First published in the UK by Scholastic Ltd, 2008

Text copyright © Terry Deary, 2008
Cover illustration copyright © Martin Brown, 2008
Illustrations copyright © Martin Brown, Geri Ford, 2008
All rights reserved

ISBN 978 1407 10305 1

Printed and bound by Tien Wah Press Pte. Ltd, Malaysia

2 4 6 8 10 9 7 5 3 1

The right of Terry Deary, Martin Brown and Geri Ford to be identified as the author and
illustrators of this work respectively has been asserted by them in accordance with the Copyright,
Designs and Patents Act, 1988.

Introduction

You really should NOT be reading this book. And if you ARE reading it just make sure no grumpy grown-up or toffee-nosed teacher catches you. Because this book is packed with the worst people in the history of the world. Villains.

'VILLAIN' – A BAD PERSON WHO HARMS OTHER PEOPLE OR BREAKS THE LAW' ... OOOOH!

But even worse, this is a 'handbook'...

'HANDBOOK' – A BOOK WITH INSTRUCTIONS OR ADVICE ABOUT HOW TO DO SOMETHING ... OOOOH!

So, if this is a handbook on 'Villains' you can expect to get some 'advice' on how to be a villain! You can see why awkward adults would not want you to read it, can't you? Sweet, harmless little you could turn into a monstrous maniac by page 96.

Why would you want to be a villain? Maybe because villains seem to have more fun ... they beat and bully, cut and carve, rob and raid, stab and steal, torture and terrify.

---

1 Mind you, other words for villain are not as kind as 'bad person'. If you become a villain, a wordbook called a thesaurus says you could also be called: creep, dirty dog, monkey, rapscallion, sleazeball, slime bucket or – nicest of all – snot!

Of course most of the villains in history have come to nasty ends. So it's only fair to warn you that if you DO follow the handbook you will probably end up a horrible villain who is horribly dead.

Take Adolf Hitler, for example. One of the greatest villains ended up DOUBLE dead – he swallowed poison then shot himself. (I wonder why he didn't shoot himself then take poison?)

There have even been villains in history, like Rasputin, who ended up double-double dead! And that is tricky to manage.

Here is a horrible history of horrible people. Just don't get caught reading it. You have been warned!

'WARMED' – MADE A COMFORTABLE HIGH TEMPERATURE, ALTHOUGH NOT HOT? UH?

I said WARNED, not warmed, meathead.

SO–RR–EEEE!

Many Villains were just nasty from the moment they were born. If you want to be a top terror, it helps to be born a villain and to grow up doing villainous things from an early age.

1 EMPEROR ELAGABALUS, Roman emperor (AD 203–222)

This terrible tot's mummy made him the high priest of Elagabalus, the sun god. That meant he sacrificed hundreds of sheep and cattle in the temple and then poured rich wine over the blood-dripping bodies.

Yummy.

So he grew up a bit 'odd'. After a while the sad lad really began to believe he WAS the sun god and changed his name to Elagabalus. You wouldn't believe the things he did. Or would you?

Lousy life

Can you match up these bits of Elagabalus's nasty life?

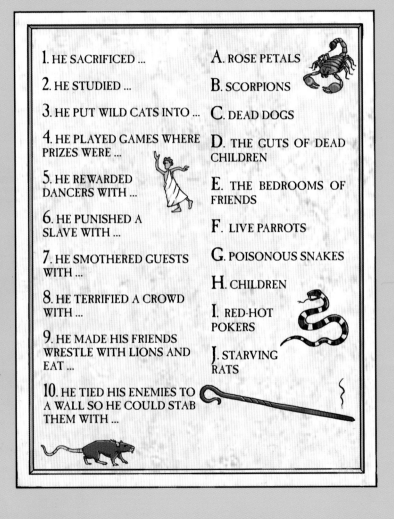

1. HE SACRIFICED ...

2. HE STUDIED ...

3. HE PUT WILD CATS INTO ...

4. HE PLAYED GAMES WHERE PRIZES WERE ...

5. HE REWARDED DANCERS WITH ...

6. HE PUNISHED A SLAVE WITH ...

7. HE SMOTHERED GUESTS WITH ...

8. HE TERRIFIED A CROWD WITH ...

9. HE MADE HIS FRIENDS WRESTLE WITH LIONS AND EAT ...

10. HE TIED HIS ENEMIES TO A WALL SO HE COULD STAB THEM WITH ...

A. ROSE PETALS

B. SCORPIONS

C. DEAD DOGS

D. THE GUTS OF DEAD CHILDREN

E. THE BEDROOMS OF FRIENDS

F. LIVE PARROTS

G. POISONOUS SNAKES

H. CHILDREN

I. RED-HOT POKERS

J. STARVING RATS

Answers:

1H) He started to sacrifice children in the temples but he only killed children who had still had TWO parents so there was twice the misery.

2D) He paraded the guts of sacrificed children in golden bowls and examined them so he could see into the future.

3E) He slipped bears and wild cats into guests' bedrooms as they slept.

4B) He played games where prizes were gold or lettuce leaves, diamonds or scorpions.

5C) He rewarded some dancing girls with dead dogs hung around their necks.

6J) He ordered a slave to collect 500 kilos of spiders' webs – the slave failed and was eaten alive by starving rats.

7A) He had a trick ceiling in his dining room. It opened up to flood the room with rose and violet petals – but these suffocated the guests.

8G) He gathered crowds to watch a show – then scattered poisonous snakes so that people would be bitten or trampled in the panic.

9F) The young 'god' invited friends to dinner and made them wrestle with lions and eat live parrots.

10I) His enemies were tied to a wall so he could stab them with red-hot pokers. Strips of skin were torn off them and they were dipped in salty water.

2 TAMERLANE THE GREAT, Mongol warrior (1336–1405)

Tamerlane himself was meant to be a ruthless ruler from the second he was born. How did his

RATTLE
RATTLE

family know? Because baby Tamerlane was born with blood-filled hands. A deadly sign. A blood clot in the cot!

Sure enough his hands were steeped in blood for the rest of his life. His favourite building was a tower made from the skulls of his victims. All right if you have a head for heights. BOOM! BOOM!

3 IVAN THE TERRIBLE, Russian ruler (1530–84)

Ivan was terrible even when he was a kid. His hobby was torturing animals and he liked throwing dogs off the roof of the Kremlin palace. If he could catch a bird then he would tear out every feather and poke out each eye before slitting it open. As for a spider, he'd pull off each leg and watch it spin round, helpless.

Ivan's enemy Prince Boris Telupa was spiked on a wooden pole – he took 15 hours to die, talking all the while to his mother who had been forced to watch.

Ivan carried a wooden pole with a metal spike on to lash out at people who annoyed him. One day he lashed out at his own son and killed him.

4 JULIUS CAESAR of Austria (1585–1609)

Julius started young … attacking servants with a knife. One servant died. His dad had him locked away for a while … good servants are hard to find. When Julius was released a lot of the other servants ran away.

> DID I SAY SOMETHING TO UPSET THEM?

Julius didn't get any better. He attacked his girlfriend with a knife and threw her out of his window. She landed in the castle pond.

When the girl returned Julius went mad. He…

➡ stabbed her.
➡ cut off her ears.
➡ gouged out one eye.
➡ smashed out her teeth.
➡ split her skull.
➡ threw pieces of her flesh all around the room.

She died. After three hours he recovered from his frenzy and ordered her wrapped in linen and carried away. He personally nailed down the lid of her coffin.

This time Julius's dad had him locked away for good.

5 MURAD IV, ruler of the Ottoman Empire (1612–40)

Murad IV of Turkey was five years old when his father died. Six years later he took the throne from his potty uncle, Mad Mustapha.

Here are 10 foul facts about Murad … but ONE of them is a lie! Which one?

1. Eleven-year-old Murad hated his Grand Vezir (what we'd call a Prime Minister) and had him executed.

2. THEN Murad wanted the Vezir's friends killed. All 500 of them. They were strangled.

3. His guards set off round Baghdad, looking for spies, and Murad said, 'If you find one, kill him – or her. No trial. Find and kill'.

4. He gave his history teacher detention – hanging him in a cage without food and water till he died.

5. He ordered his guards to kill his brother.

6. He fought endless wars. In Baghdad in 1638 his men massacred 30,000 soldiers and then 30,000 women and children inside the city.

7. Murad's musician was executed for playing a song from Persia – the enemy.

8. And then Murad banned smoking, booze and coffee. The punishment was death.

YOU SHOULD READ THE PACKET ... IT SAYS, 'SMOKING KILLS'!

9. He once came across a group of women singing in a meadow and having a picnic. 'I hate that noise,' he said. 'Drown them in the river.'

10. At night he wandered the streets in his nightshirt and killed anyone he saw. He really liked chopping the heads off men with fat necks.

Answer: Fact 4 is false. Yes, it's a nice idea ... but it didn't happen.

---

6 CAPTAIN RICHARD DUDLEY, highwayman (1681–1708)

How on EARTH do you start being a villain? Richard Dudley would tell you…

7 BILLY THE KID (1859–81)

William Bonney (or Billy the Kid) really was a kid when he went to the pub with his mum aged 12.

A man in the bar insulted Billy's mum … probably said, 'Mrs Bonney you're as bonny as a baboon's bottom.'

Billy drew a knife and stabbed the man to death.

Do NOT try this in your local pub because a) you will make a right mess on the carpet and b) your mum will probably send you to bed with no tea and no television.

Billy was a villain…

WANTED

· BILLY THE KID ·

KNOWN TO HAVE KILLED SHERIFF JAMES BRADY

Who was a crook and deserved it!

GUILTY OF

CATTLE RUSTLING, ROBBERY AND MURDER

SLIM, 5 FOOT 8 INCHES. ENJOYS DANCING *sure do!*

Billy had a friend called Pat Garrett. Pat Garrett was made sheriff of Lincoln County and had the job of hunting down Billy. Billy was caught and sentenced to hang for killing Sheriff Brady.

Billy killed his prison guards and escaped. Pal Pat tracked him down and before you could say, 'Hello, old mate,' he shot Billy the Kid dead.

No more escapes.

Billy had 19 notches on his gun – one for every man he'd killed.

Killer conquerors

In history there have been villains who didn't just mess about with the odd murder, they were complete massacring maniacs! They invaded countries and put a stoppo to the oppo by killing countrywide.

If these villains went in for skull exams then who would come top of the pile?

1 Attila the Hun, leader of the Huns (AD 406–453)

Attila smashed the Romans and anyone else who got in his way.

• He massacred a city full of people to teach his enemies a lesson.

• Terrible tales were told of him eating human flesh.

• He used attack-dogs to tear enemy armies apart.

• He wrecked the graveyards of his dead enemies.

• But the most gruesome was the story that his wife, Gudhrun, served him with the hearts of his two sons Erp and Eitil for dinner.

What could stop awful Attila and his horrible Huns?

A nose-bleed. He got married, his nose started to bleed and he choked to death on his own blood.

IF I'D KNOWN I WOULDN'T HAVE WORN WHITE!

SORRY DEAR!

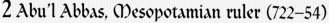

2 Abu'l Abbas, Mesopotamian ruler (722–54)

His nickname was 'Shedder of Blood'. Would you have dinner with this man? His enemies did. He massacred them, then went on with dinner – over their dead bodies.

He also dug up the corpses of dead enemies and had them flogged and scattered to be eaten by wild animals. Tasty treats.

3 Genghis Khan, Mongol warrior (1162–1227)

Ruthless raider. Genghis had a nice motto you might like to follow: 'The deafeated must die so the winners may be happy'. In other words, 'I'm not murdering you because I'm nasty – I'm doing it because it will make me happy'.

In the town of Merv, Khan ordered his army to kill a million people … in a single day.

4 Tamerlane, Mongol warrior (1336–1405)

Enjoyed conquering new lands – and then having the odd massacre of the conquered people. When he invaded India he travelled to Delhi. He massacred 100,000 Hindu prisoners. Why? Because it was too much trouble to feed them and guard them.

5 Vlad Tepes, ruler of Wallachia (1431–76)

The real Count Dracula was even more vicious than the vampire in the stories. Vlad used to take his prisoners of war and stick each of them on top of a sharpened pole. The poles were then arranged around his camp and he enjoyed a tasty dinner while the victims screamed and died all around him. Something to liven up school dinners, perhaps?

One of his nastiest tricks was to capture a group of prisoners of war. He had three of them fried alive. The others were then forced to eat them.

6 Pachacuti, Inca emperor (1438–71)

Pachacuti's name meant 'he who shakes the Earth'. And he shook the Chanca tribes in Peru with his cruelty. The Inca emperor took the defeated Chanca leaders and stuffed their skins with straw and ashes. The scarecrow corpses were taken to a special burial ground and seated on stone benches. The stuffed arms were bent so that when the wind blew the dead fingers beat the stretched skin on their bellies like drums!

His warriors went into battle with this cheerful song about chicha beer…

> *We'll drink chicha from your skull*
> *From your teeth we'll make a necklace*
> *From your bones we'll make our flutes*
> *From your skin we'll make a drum*
> *And then we'll dance.*

7 Francisco Solano Lopez, Paraguayan leader (died 1870)

Lopez saw himself as the 'Napoleon' of South America and even walked around with a hand stuck in his jacket the way the French Emperor Napoleon used to do.

Lopez sent his armies into hopeless battles where they were wiped out. So many died there were just 221,000 people left in Paraguay out of 1,337,000 when Lopez came into power.

THERE'S NO ONE LEFT TO WASH MY UNDERPANTS

DIV

8 Leopold II, King of Belgium (1835–1909)

Ruthless ruler who was only interested in making money from his African colonies. His soldiers ruled the Africans through terror and bullying. They sliced off the noses, ears and hands of rebels and shot women and babies. Never mind, it all went to make Leo the richest man in the world.

9 Josef Stalin, Russian leader (1879–1953)

Probably to blame for the deaths of 50 million people – most of them the Russian people on his side! That probably makes him the greatest killer in all history.

His secret police and army wiped out anyone who stood in his way. But he won World War II so no one said too much about his nasty little life. 'Winners' get away with it.

10 Adolf Hitler, German leader (1889–1945)

Germany was in a mess after losing World War I and wanted a strong man to lead them. Hitler had potty ideas but the Germans believed him.

He said the Jews were to blame for Germany's defeat. They believed him. He said the answer was to massacre the Jews. The Germans believed him. They killed 6 million. But Hitler lost the war and shot himself. No great loss; just a shame he didn't do it 20 years earlier.

MILLIONS OF DOLLARS

MILLIONS OF BODIES

Vicious villain tip 2:
Get a gang

It's not a lot of fun being a lonely villain but if you get a gang of cut-throats and bullies they can do the hard work for you. Of course it doesn't always work...

Eustace the monk (1170–1217)

Eustace was a French monk, but he left the monastery to kill the men who had murdered his father. He became an avenging outlaw and gathered a gang of villains around him.

Eustace had a strange way of dealing with the victims he robbed. He asked them...

HOW MUCH MONEY DO YOU HAVE?

If you told the truth he let you keep it. If you lied he took everything.

Eustace was loyal to his men. An enemy war band gouged out the eyes of some of his men. Eustace chopped off the feet of four men who did the gouging. The Bible says, 'An eye for an eye.' Eustace believed in a foot for an eye.

It was said Eustace the Monk had special, black magic powers. He could make monks in the monastery do botty-burps whenever he wanted!

Imagine if you could do that! The fun you could have in a History lesson … or a school assembly.

Another Eustace trick was to use disguises to escape capture or spy on his enemies. He tried…

fishmonger

pastry cook

carpenter

crippled beggar

leper

shepherd

peasant

pilgrim

Eustace was a great warrior and – because he hated the French who killed his dad – fought for King John of England.

At last he caught his father's killers. One man was made to twist his own rope before hanging himself from a tree.

Then, in 1205, Eustace switched sides and fought for France. The traitor. He became a pirate, attacking English ships. The English finally captured him in 1217 after a sea battle near the coast of Kent. Eustace's ship was carrying a 'trebuchet' (a large war catapult) on the deck.

Eustace was given a choice…

DO YOU WANT TO BE BEHEADED ON THE SHIP'S RAIL OR ON THE TREBUCHET?

TOUGH QUESTION. WANNA GIVE ME A FEW WEEKS TO THINK ABOUT IT? A FEW YEARS MAYBE?

Eustace was beheaded on the trebuchet.

Foul Friar Tuk (1420s)

In February 1416 the counties of Surrey and Sussex were in a panic. A gang was rampaging around and killing deer in the forest. The foresters tried to stop the gang but had their houses burned down. And the leader of the gang was a foul friar with a familiar name…

WANTED

Dead or alive
(or a bit of both)

The gang led by the foul friar[2] known as

Friar Tuk
for

Burning cottages and killing deer

Big reward for info on this fire friar

Yes, BIG reward - you'll eat well

In fact, you can tuck in ...

if you help get Tuk out

HA! NOTHING LIKE ME

Was this the famous Friar Tuck who later made his name as a member of Robin Hood's gang? Probably not. The name was just added to the Robin Hood stories.

It turned out Friar Tuk was a Sussex priest whose real name was Richard Stafford. A deer man.

In the end the law gave up trying to catch Tuk and gave him a pardon.

2 A friar is a travelling monk, not the man in the local fish shop who cooks your chips – he is a fryer. A friar would just travel around preaching – or in Friar Tuk's case, nicking things.

James Dalton (1700–30)

Little Jim was a street robber in London. When he was five years old his dad was arrested and sentenced to hang. Mr Dalton said...

> I WANT YOU TO HANG AROUND AND WATCH ME BEING EXECUTED, SON

> YOU HANG AROUND, I'LL WATCH

James was a pickpocket at first. Then he joined a violent gang near St Paul's Cathedral in London.

The gang smashed their way into houses and robbed people. Big mistake. The law officers offered a reward for their capture ... when one member of the gang was arrested he made sure the others were arrested too.

> THAT'S THE TROUBLE WITH BEING IN A GANG – ONE GETS CAUGHT AND YOU ALL HANG

The Irish Hellfire Club (1735)

Some gangs were just for foul fun! The Irish Hellfire Club was for posh young men who wanted to run wild and cruel. Members were known as 'Bucks'. They met at The Eagle Tavern in Dublin's city centre – how eerie is that. (Eyrie ... eerie geddit? Oh, never mind.)

Sometime they met at Montpelier Hill outside the city and away from the eyes of the Irish law. Some say they had sacrifices. Ghostly black cats are still seen there today! Why? Did they sacrifice black cats? Or were they white cats just badly burned by rotten cooks? One report says they killed a dwarf – but there are no ghostly dwarfs there to tell the tale.

One member, Richard Chappell Whaley, was known as 'Burn Chapel' from his Sunday morning habit of going round and setting fire to thatched Catholic churches.

The members' most disgusting habit was drinking 'scultheen', a mixture of whiskey and rotten butter.

One of their more gruesome games was to slit open the nostrils of their victims. Why? Who nose?

'Little' Harpe (1770–1803) and 'Big' Harpe (1768–99)

The Harpe Brothers were murderous outlaws in America. They were probably the first serial killers as we know them today.

They fled from Knoxville, Tennessee, when they were accused of murdering a man named Johnson. His body was found in a river, ripped open and weighted with stones. This was a popular trick of the Harpes.

The brothers killed at least 40 men, women and children on the Wild West frontier.

An enemy called Stigall caught up with the killers and shot 'Big' Harpe. He cut off his head and stuck it on a pole. The place where this happened is still known as 'Harpe's Head.'

'Little' Harpe escaped. He teamed up with the villainous Samuel Mason (1739–1803), who robbed boats with his gang on the Mississippi. But they fell out. 'Little Harpe' beheaded Sam Mason and used his head to claim the reward.

But someone in the crowd pointed out that he was 'Little' Harpe. Harpe was hung and his head was stuck on a pole next to Mason's.

SERVES YOU RIGHT

Ben Hall (1837–65)

Ben Hall is sometimes seen as the Robin Hood of Australia – an outlaw with a heart of gold. He and his merry men robbed ten coaches and never killed anyone.

Why not? Depends who you want to believe.

Friend of Ben Hall

BEN KILLED NO ONE BECAUSE HE WAS A GENTLEMAN

Enemy of Ben Hall

BEN KILLED NO ONE BECAUSE HE WAS A TERRIBLE SHOT

Ben wounded several people and once tried to murder a policeman – so who do YOU believe?

The police tracked Ben to Billabong Creek and wounded him. He told his friend…

SHOOT ME DEAD, BILLY! DON'T LET THE COPS TAKE ME ALIVE

We don't know if Billy did finish him off ... but Ben Hall's body was found with THIRTY-SIX bullets in it. Police bullets? They can't all have been Billy bullets, can they?

BANG! THIRTY-FOUR BANG! THIRTY-FIVE BANG!

ALL RIGHT! ALL RIGHT! I THINK THAT'S WHAT THEY CALL OVERKILL, BILL

Butch Cassidy and the Sundance Kid (1890s)

Butch's Wild Bunch was the last of the American outlaw gangs. A young cowboy joined who had already served term in jail at Sundance – so he got the name 'Sundance Kid'. But the gang wasn't as cheerful and harmless as it sounded.

• These rustlers built cabins and corrals at the end of a desolate valley called Hole in the Wall, near Kaycee, Wyoming, a natural fortress with caves, with a narrow entrance which was always guarded. This is why the gang is sometimes referred to as the 'Hole in the Wall Gang'.

• In the outlaw town of Star Valley, there was a saloon where the back wall was papered with stolen dollar bills. All friends of Butch's got their drinks free in this saloon.

• The gang weren't that bright. No one in the gang knew they had a private detective agent in their midst – Charles Siringo. He had joined the gang pretending to be an old, grizzled outlaw on the run for murder and had been accepted. He gathered enough information to spoil several planned robberies.

The Barker family (early 1930s)

If you can't find any friends to form a gang then join up with your family. That's what Americans Herman, Lloyd, Arthur and Fred Barker did.

And who was the gang leader? Their dear old mum, Ma Barker, of course.

They robbed banks and post offices, but most of all they kidnapped. They made $3 million, although at least 10 people died. The gang became known as … 'The Bloody Barkers'. The banks put out an unusual 'wanted' notice…

WANTED
THE BLOODY BARKERS
$5000
REWARD
FOR THESE
DEAD BANK ROBBERS
The banks will not pay one cent for live bank robbers

One by one the Barkers were captured, till at last just Ma and Fred were caught in their home. The law used tear-gas bombs, machine-guns and rifles. After a 45-minute gun battle Ma and Fred were dead. Ma was still clutching her machine-gun.

Al Capone (1899–1947)

Al Capone was America's most famous gangster in the 1920s. Two of Al's killers, Anesimi and Scalise, agreed to turn on their boss and kill him.

Big Al heard about their plot and planned a suitable revenge.

Capone arranged a big dinner party where Anesimi and Scalise were the main guests. Al gave a speech and talked about how important it was to be loyal to your boss.

Then he had Anesimi and Scalise tied to their chairs. He took out a baseball bat and, in front of his guests, battered the heads of the traitors till they were dead.

If that's not enough to put you off you dinner, what is?

John Dillinger (1903–34)

Dillinger was famous as the leader of an American bank-robbing gang. The head of the police hunting him (J Edgar Hoover) gave Dillinger the famous title…

PUBLIC ENEMY NUMBER ONE!

WANTED

Dillinger was arrested in 1933 and the gang showed how useful a gang can be. Three of them dressed up as prison officers, walked into the jail and set boss Dillinger free.

His next gang had the famous 'Baby Face' Nelson and other violent robbers. He was betrayed by a girlfriend who took the $10,000 reward.

Dillinger was gunned down.

It was the end of the gangster age in the USA.

Terrible torturers

Some of the nastiest villains seem to have enjoyed making others suffer – and for others, torturing was their full-time job. You kill someone and that's it. When they die the fun ends. But kill someone s-l-o-w-l-y and the fun goes on as long as they do.

1 Emperor Tiberius of Rome (ruled AD 14–37)

This bad-tempered man was easily upset. And if you upset him he'd have your ears cut off and fed to his lions.

He became so annoyed with one of his wives that he had her put into the bathroom. The servants were ordered to turn up the heat. She was steamed to death.

2 Emperor Domitian of Rome (ruled AD 81–96)

Daft Domitian became madder and crueller the longer he ruled. He loved to torture men to death. One of his favourite nasty tricks was to chain the victim to a wall. Then the emperor would hold a flaming torch under the man's naughty bits before cutting them off.

He then watched as the poor man bled to death.

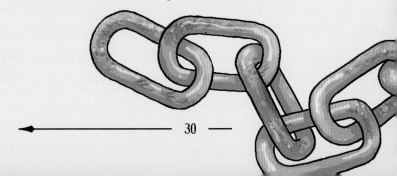

3 Earl Godwin, Anglo-Saxon Earl of Wessex (1001–53)

Poor little Prince Alfred wanted to be king after the Danish King Cnut died in 1036. But villainous Earl Godwin, Anglo-Saxon Earl of Wessex, had other ideas. The Anglo-Saxon Chronicle reported the event but it's a bit dull to read. If the miserable monks had been potty poets it might have looked like this...

Prince Alfred was a cheerful lad, with eyes of sparkling blue,
Till Godwin had his eyes put out, yes both! Not one, but two!
He sent the blinded prince away to be a monk in Ely.
There the little Alfie died; did Godwin care? Not really.

Then Godwin set about the slaying of Alf's friends.
He had them caught and had them brought to really sticky ends.
Some he sold as slaves for cash and some he scalped their head,
Others he locked up in chains and some he killed stone dead.

Some he had their hands chopped off or arms or legs or ears.
No wonder they all fled (or tried to flee) in fear.
We've never seen a crueller deed been done in all our land
Since those dread Vikings came and took peace from our hands.

The Anglo-Saxons believed that God took revenge on villains. 'An eye for an eye' the Bible said. So Alfie would be pleased to know that Godwin's son, Harold, died at the battle of Hastings 30 years later ... with an arrow in his eye!

4 Alexander 'the Wolf of Badenoch' (1343–1405)

Awful Alex ruled the north of Scotland and had a nasty habit of hunting in the Rothiemurchus Forest. He set fire to parts of it to drive out the deer and kill them. But he also enjoyed hunting outlaws this way.

When he caught a victim he had them locked in a cellar with a metre of icy water.

If the prisoner stood up they would live – if they tried to sit down or fell asleep, they would drown. They were left there for two or three days. If they lived then they were set free.

✖ DID YOU KNOW...? ✖

Villains could be fastened in the 'stocks' – their feet were trapped in a wooden block. People could come and throw rubbish at them ... or stones!

But in 1384, at Sarum Gaol, a prisoner was kept so long in the stocks, his feet rotted away.

MY FEET WERE IN THE STOCKS TOO LONG

MY FEET WERE IN MY SOCKS TOO LONG

---

5 Vlad II of Romania (1390–1447)

The real Count Dracula, Vlad III of Romania, was horribly cruel. BUT … they were cruel times. Look what happened to Vlad's dad, Vlad II!

Vlad II was assassinated by means of scalping - 'scalping', for the Turks, meant cutting the edges of the face and pulling the face's skin off … while the person was still alive and awake.

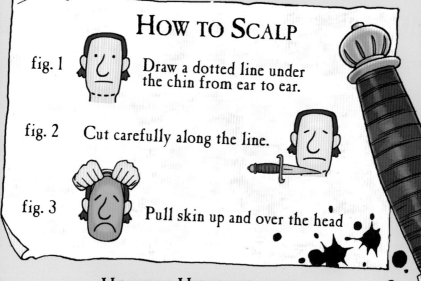

HOW TO SCALP

fig. 1   Draw a dotted line under the chin from ear to ear.

fig. 2   Cut carefully along the line.

fig. 3   Pull skin up and over the head

HORRIBLE HISTORIES NOTE:
Do NOT practise this using your own dad!
(Use an old history teacher instead.)

6 Tomas de Torquemada, Spanish torturer (1420–98)

A Christian monk. Surely this was a peaceful enough job? No, he decided Jews were dangerous people and he would torture people to discover who were good Christians and who were not.

The Church said Tom's torturers must not spill any of their victims' blood. So what did they do?

• Used thumbscrews to squeeze their fingernails.

• Tore their flesh with white-hot irons (to 'seal' the wound before blood could flow).

• Roasted them over fires.

• Forced water down their throats till they almost drowned.

• Hung them from the ceiling by their wrists and put weights on their feet.

• The ones who lived through the torture were usually burned.

WEIGHT FOR HIM

7 György Dózsa, hungarian rebel (died 1514)

To the people György Dózsa was a Christian hero – to the posh horrible Hungarians he was a dangerous criminal.

He stuck his enemies on the sharp point of a pole and let them die slowly. That led to the ancient *Horrible Histories* joke…

ALL RIGHT … I GET THE POINT!

I KNEW HE WAS GOING TO SAY THAT!

SO PREDICTABLE

Sometimes György Dózsa crucified them. Thousands died. So when he was captured you can be sure his enemies had a special treat waiting for him.

He was sat on a heated iron throne with a red-hot iron crown on his head and a hot sceptre in his hand (mocking his plans to be king). While Dózsa was suffering, he was set upon and eaten by six other rebels, who had been starved.

Villain? Or victim? Or both?

8 Elizabeth Branch (1687–1740)

You don't have to be a ruler to be a torturer. Elizabeth Branch was just a rich woman – filthy rich.

Lousy Liz used to catch flies and kill them and loved to torment dogs and cats. When she married she taught her daughter Betty cruel ways. Betty often cut open live mice and birds, torturing them for three hours before they died[3].

> WELL DONE SWEETHEART, THAT'S LOVELY MUTILATING

• Liz and Betty began tormenting the servants. One servant said the Branch family forced him to eat his own poo.
• Another 13-year-old servant was late so the brutal Branches beat her with rods, broomsticks and shoes for seven hours ... till she died. (Then they stopped.)
• At the trial they even managed to kick some of the witnesses!
• The Branches were hanged. The people of the village hated Liz and Betty. They would have torn their bodies apart at the hanging – so the cruel couple were hanged at 6 a.m. before most people were out of bed.

3 Liz got the idea from reading about Emperor Nero who (her books said) 'ripped up his mother's belly to see how he was born' ... which just goes to show how dangerous reading history books can be! Don't do it! Burn this book at once ... so long as you've paid for it.

Vicious villains' tool kit

If you want to be a villain you need some cool kit to help. Here are a few tips from history...

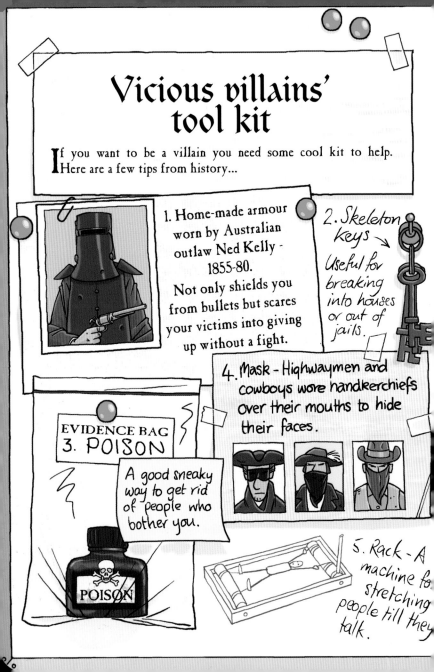

1. Home-made armour worn by Australian outlaw Ned Kelly - 1855-80.
Not only shields you from bullets but scares your victims into giving up without a fight.

2. Skeleton keys →
Useful for breaking into houses or out of jails.

4. Mask - Highwaymen and cowboys wore handkerchiefs over their mouths to hide their faces.

EVIDENCE BAG
3. POISON

A good sneaky way to get rid of people who bother you.

POISON

5. Rack - A machine for stretching people till they talk.

6. Skull

Build a pyramid with them if you're Tamerlane, or they make good drinking cups for Crusader knights. Nadir Shah of Persia 1688-1747 had towers built from the skulls of his victims.

7. Notepad.

Kidnappers can write ransom notes and killers can write letters to the police

plod →

8. Car.

Great for getaways after you've robbed a bank - but it has to be faster than the cop cars.

9. Flintlock pistol.

The flintlock pistol was invented around 1638 and was great for highwaymen. Now they had a weapon they could hold in one hand while they held their horse's reins in the other.

10. Camera

Take your photo if you want to be a famous villain. Send it to the papers.

NASTY NOTES

1 Nutcase Ned FORGOT to make leg armour. So the law officers simply shot him in the shins. Result ... Kelly caught. And his armour didn't save him when they hanged him.

2 The villain Jack Sheppard (1702–24) broke out of every jail they tried to keep him in and every set of chains. In the end they caught him because he was too drunk to run away.

3 An Arab chemist invented the deadly white powder arsenic. It became a murderer's favourite because it had little taste and could be mixed with sugar, so you could pop it in your victim's tea. And a doctor would often say the victim died naturally of 'gastric fever'!

4 Of course it also makes it easy to blow your nose!

5 It was popular with Tudor torturers. The famous plotter Guy Fawkes was stretched on the rack till his arms and legs were almost torn out. He survived – only to be hanged, drawn and quartered.

6 In 1119 crusader Count Robert was captured in battle and taken before the Atabeg of Damascus. The Atabeg drew his sword and cut off Robert's head. As if that wasn't cruel enough he threw the crusader's body to the dogs but kept his skull. It was encrusted with jewels and used as a drinking cup!

General Kitchener of Britain also used his enemy's skull as an inkwell.

7 In 1888 Jack the Ripper wrote to the police and made fun of them. He called himself 'Jack the Ripper' but never gave his real name – that is a GOOD idea. We still don't know who he was.

8 The Dillinger gang in the USA used cars after a robbery. In 1934 they robbed a bank in one state then drove across the border into the next state. Police weren't allowed to arrest people across the border – so they just let them go!

9 Highwaymen were a terror on the roads from the 1600s when they robbed coaches. They disappeared in Victorian times when trains were invented. Trains are harder to catch – especially on a horse.

10 American gangsters like Bonnie and Clyde and John Dillinger were popular because they had their pictures taken and the public loved it. Mind you, they ended up very dead.

Vicious villain tip 3:
Think BIG

A villain may mug his granny for the 10p in her purse, but that's just a start. A real villain has b-i-g ideas and wants to smash and rob the whole world.

1 King Herod the Great (74–4 BC)

Herod was King of Judea (South Palestine) and his last years were a reign of terror.

He heard that a baby had been born who would become King of the Jews. He didn't know WHICH baby. So Herod decided to think BIG.

EASY. WE SIMPLY KILL ALL THE BABIES IN THE LAND[4]. OFF YOU GO. CHOP! CHOP!

Of course the baby he was out to kill was Jesus … and Jesus escaped. (Well, he would. He had a host of angels to help him.) You weren't even safe if you were a grown-up boy … Herod had his own sons executed. Nice Dad.

2 Wu Zhao, empress of China (AD 624–705)

She started out as one of the emperor's many wives. But Wu Zhao decided to think BIG. She decided she wanted to rule the whole country.

4 Of course Herod MAY have said, 'Kill all the baby boys in Bethlehem.' That would be just a handful, not hundreds.

She ruled for 15 years. Then her son returned from abroad and threw her off the throne. She died … but she was aged 80, so she hadn't done badly.

3 Basil Bulgaroctonus, Byzantine emperor (958–1025)

Basil's army managed to surround the enemy forces, the Bulgars, and they surrendered. Did he spare them? Not exactly.

He blinded the whole Bulgar army … not one or two leaders. Oh, no, Bas thought BIG. He blinded every enemy soldier, EXCEPT he left one eye to each 100th man, so that the soldiers might be led back to their king, Samuel.

Sad Sam died of shock shortly after seeing this terrible spectacle. The blinded Bulgar army would never go home to be teachers – no pupils, you see?

4 Christopher Columbus (1451–1506)

Christopher Columbus discovered America in 1492.

When he set off for home he kidnapped around 20 Indians. The terrible conditions on the ships meant only seven arrived in Spain alive. They were enough to show the Spanish that these strong Indians would make great slaves.

Columbus headed back to America – and this time he had over 1,200 soldiers armed with guns, swords, cannon and attack-dogs. And he wasn't going for a holiday – Disneyworld hadn't been invented. He was going back for more slaves.

In 1495 the Spanish rounded up 500 Arawak Indians on Haiti to be sent back to Spain and took another 500 to work for them on the islands. Half the slaves died on the journey but Cruel Chris shrugged and said...

Although they die now they will not always die. We can send all the slaves from here that you can sell!

He thought BIG. But he was wrong. Forced work and dreadful diseases killed all the Arawaks off in time. The Indians weren't allowed to say, 'No!' An Indian who disobeyed would have his (or her) nose cut off or his ears lopped. Then they were sent back to the village as a warning to the others.

They were packed into ships like sardines on supermarket shelves. They were locked in to stop them escaping and died in the filthy, scorching air. Spanish history writer Peter Martyr said you didn't need a compass to find your way along the slave ship routes...

All you had to do was follow the trail of dead Indians that had to be thrown overboard.

When they ran out of Indian slaves the Spanish started capturing them in Africa and taking them across the Atlantic to work in America. Cruel Chris began the terrible slave trade that lasted another 400 years.

5 Tizoc, Aztec emperor (died 1486)

When Emperor Tizoc wanted a sacrifice he believed that he needed 20 warriors to die on the pyramid in Tenochtitlan. Then he decided to terrify all the other tribes in Mexico with a huge massacre. He took every single man from three Mixtec tribes, 20,000 men, and sent them for sacrifice.

That's thinking BIG.

The victims had eagle feathers stuck to them with their own blood and were led to the Aztec capital. They were all killed on the pyramid. The Aztec warriors killed the first ones, then the priests took over. In early sacrifices the people had eaten small parts of the victims. This time there were too many. They were simply killed and their bodies thrown into the marshes.

It terrified the other tribes in Mexico all right, but it also disgusted them. They learned to hate the Aztecs. They knew they would have to wait, but one day their chance would come to overthrow the vicious heart-ripping people. And it did.

6 Captain Thomas Blood, jewel thief (1618–80)

No one can steal the English Crown Jewels from the Tower of London. They are the most closely-guarded valuables in the toughest of towers.

But Irish villain Thomas Blood thought big. Blood made friends with the keeper of the jewels, Talbot Edwards, and got himself invited to dinner. He tied up the keeper, stuffed some jewels down his trousers and rode off. He was caught by a guard as he was almost out of the gates and free.

Blood was caught but said, 'I will speak to no one but King Charles II himself'.

Blood was taken before the King, who decided he liked a man with such big ideas.

Charles forgave him and gave him a pension of £500 a year. Lucky Blood.

Colonel Blood had the cheek to tell the King that…

THE CROWN JEWELS AREN'T REALLY WORTH THAT MUCH. PEOPLE SAID THEY ARE WORTH £100,000 – I WOULDN'T GIVE £6,000 FOR THEM

Charles was amused and released the thief. Why would the King do that? Some people believe Charles II set up the whole thing – that he planned to steal his own jewels and sell them.

Not only did Blood get an Irish estate from Charles, he was also welcomed into the royal court where he was a popular figure. He was admired as the man who almost stole the Crown Jewels … and Talbot Edwards was almost as famous as the man who nearly lost them.

But Blood went to his grave with some vicious words on his tombstone:

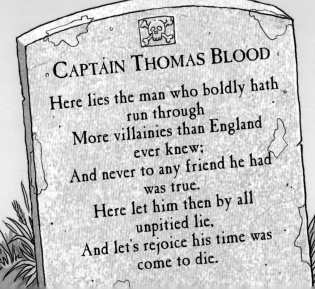

CAPTAIN THOMAS BLOOD

Here lies the man who boldly hath run through
More villainies than England ever knew;
And never to any friend he had was true.
Here let him then by all unpitied lie,
And let's rejoice his time was come to die.

Wicked women

Villains have usually been men. But don't despair you female fans. Females CAN become villains too. Some women have made a really good job of it.

1 Cleopatra VII, Queen of Egypt (69–30 BC)

Cleo shared the throne of Egypt with her little brother Ptolemy XIII. After she met top Roman ruler Julius Caesar she didn't need little brother – and little brother was discovered drowned. Cleo married her other little brother, Ptolemy XIV, and guess what? Ptolemy was murdered. Wonder who could have arranged that?

Caesar came to a sticky end, so Cleo moved on to Roman general Mark Antony, but they lost a war against Rome. The famous story is she killed herself, bitten by a poison snake … an asp. It's tricky killing yourself that way.

HONESTLY– I'M JUST NOT HUNGRY. NO, REALLY … I'M FINE. COULDN'T POSSIBLY. NOT EVEN A NIBBLE. I THINK I MIGHT BE TURNING VEGETARIAN ANYWAY

YOU'RE BEING A PAIN IN THE ASP

BUT *Horrible Histories* can tell you…

No one wrote about Cleo's death at the time it happened. The story of the asp was written a hundred years after she died. Maybe Cleo DIDN'T kill herself – maybe she was murdered by her enemies.

2 Lucretia Borgia, Italian duchess (1480–1519)

Lucretia is supposed to be one of the deadliest women ever to have lived.

It is SAID that Lucretia wore a ring that was filled with poison. Her husband's enemies were invited to a meeting and she served them wine – then slipped in the poison[5].

But some historians think tales of lousy Lucretia may not be true – they were mostly lies made up by the Borgias' enemies.

Her brother Cesare Borgia and their father, Pope Alexander VI, enjoyed stabbing, shooting at passers-by with a crossbow, strangling, and … most of all … poisoning.

3 Mary Tudor, Queen of England (1516–58)

Henry VIII's daughter didn't manage to kill as many people as her dad, but that's because she didn't reign as long.

Some modern historians think Mary has been treated unfairly in history books. 'She wasn't all that bad', they say. In terms of executing people her father Henry VIII was worse. It's the horrible burnings where she's the Top Tudor with a nasty habit of burning Protestants. See how they compare over the page.

---

5 When adults drink wine they clink their glasses together. That is said to be an idea from the days of the Borgias. If a little wine slops from each glass to the other, it proves the other person hasn't put poison in yours.

Terrible Tudor	Rotten Reign	Burned	Awful Average
Mary	4 years	300	75 each year
Henry VIII	38 years	81	2 each year
Henry VII	24 years	10	One every 2 years
Elizabeth	45 years	5	One every 9 years

Mary aimed to be kind by allowing the executioner to strap gunpowder to her victim's legs so they'd go with a quick 'spark-bang-splatter'. But it often didn't work. More 'spark-splutter-sizzle'.

4 Amina, queen of Nigeria (1533–1610)

This warrior queen changed the history of Nigeria. She started training to fight at 16 and went on fighting until her death nearly 60 years later. She made the roads safe for her traders and built massive forts for her people. Awesome Amina. Not a villain at all…

…except for one nasty little habit. Because she was busy making war she had no time for a full-time husband. She never married. But wherever she went and conquered, she chose a 'boyfriend' from the captured enemy. He got a lovely cuddle all night long, but little did he know Amina would have him killed the next morning.

I WILL LOVE YOU TILL THE DAY I DIE!

WELL THAT'S TRUE

5 Lady Margaret Lambourne (born 1550)

Elizabeth I had Mary Queen of Scots executed in 1587.

Lady M decided to kill Elizabeth in revenge. She dressed as a man and carried two pistols into the palace – one shot for the Queen, one for herself.

Sadly, one pistol went off early and – even sadder – it killed a peacock.

WHAT IS MY DUTY?

TO PARDON ME

The Queen admired her loyalty to Mary Queen of Scots … and pardoned her.

6 Witches of Belvoir (died 1619)

Witches were often said to work in gangs … except they called them 'covens'. They BELIEVED they could perform spells, but we know it was nonsense.

The witches of Belvoir were said to be magical murderers. When Margaret Flower was sacked from her job as a servant –

she'd been pinching stuff from her boss, the Earl of Rutland –
her mum, Joan, planned revenge...

FIRST WE TAKE THESE STOLEN GLOVES FROM THE EARL'S SON, HENRY – STICK PINS IN AND DROP THEM IN BOILING WATER ...

HENRY DIED A WEEK LATER

NOW WE TAKE THESE STOLEN GLOVES FROM THE EARL'S OTHER SON, FRANCIS – AND BURY IT IN A TOILET PIT...

IN WEEKS, YOUNG FRANCIS WAS ALSO DEAD

Margaret and four witch friends were arrested. Margaret
said...

GIVE ME BREAD. IF I AM A WITCH I WILL CHOKE ON IT.

They gave her the bread ... and she choked to death.

The remaining women then turned on each other. (That's
the problem with being in a gang – if one's in trouble they're all
in trouble.)

They were all hung at Lincoln Prison on 11 March 1619.

7 Mary Aubry (died 1688)

Mary was a French housewife, living in London. In late January 1688 the head, body, arms and legs of her husband, Denis Hobry, were discovered one by one around London. His body was behind a rubbish tip, his arms and legs in one toilet and his head in another.

Law officers put the body bits back together and showed them at St Giles Church with a sign...

Mary was arrested. She said her husband was violent and she killed him to save herself. She was shown no mercy. The woman was given the special punishment for wives who killed their husbands ... she was burned alive.

8 Hannah Dagoe (died 1763)

This heartless thief broke into Widow Hussey's room and stripped it of everything the poor woman owned. Hannah was sentenced to be hanged, but she didn't go quietly on the hanging cart. The big, tough woman struggled to get her arms free and attacked her executioner, Thomas Turlis. She said...

She punched him so hard in the chest that she flattened him. She then threw her hat, cloak, and other articles of clothing into the crowd, so the hangman couldn't sell them. At last she was overpowered and Turlis got the rope around her neck.

But before the signal was given for the cart to move off, Hannah bound a handkerchief around her own head and over her face. Then she threw herself out of the cart with such force that she broke her neck and died at once.

9 Ranavalona 1, queen of Madagascar (1782–1861)

Ranavalona was not a pretty child. She had cruel eyes like a snake. She started acting evil at a very early age … then got worse.

• She married King Radama when she was very young and poisoned him.

• Ranavalona took the throne after bumping off any rivals. She then had most of her family assassinated.

• She hated foreigners, especially the island's Christian missionaries, and drove them out.

• But many of her own people stayed Christian and needed to be dealt with. Christians were dangled over a 50-metre cliff by a rope, then asked, 'Do you worship the Queen's god or Christ?' When they answered, 'Christ,' the rope was cut.

• Anyone who owned a Bible was executed. Some victims were tied up like chickens and thrown from hilltops. If that didn't kill them they were thrown again … and again … until they did die.

• Others were dressed in the bloody skins of animals and had hunting dogs set upon them.

• Some were yoked together like cattle and left in the tangled jungles of Madagascar where they would break their necks trying to get free, or would get caught in the undergrowth and starve to death.

• But Ranavalona's favourite method of execution was to have a prisoner dropped in a pit at the bottom of a hill. Her soldiers, at the top of the hill, would tip over pots of boiling water; when the water reached the pit, it would slowly rise up and boil the prisoner alive.

• Ranavalona's people often enjoyed the sight and killing Christians became a sport for all the family to watch. One visitor wrote…

Seven Christians stood together in the bright sunlight, bound with ropes, singing a hymn. Spearmen advanced. Around them a crowd of men, women and children, more than sixty thousand strong, cheered as the spears were driven home. One by one, the men and women fell and writhed on the sandy ground, their hymn fading slowly into silence. Above the writhing bodies, on a ridge, a score of crosses stood with crucified Christians, some of whom still lived despite the day-and-a-half they had hung upon the wood.

Vicious villain tip 4:
Think new

All right, a bit of shoplifting may get a villain a new pair of knickers. But it's been done before! Great villains come up with new ways to make misery.

Top assassin tip

Want to kill a king? You can't get near them. There are always bodyguards around them.

Bodyguards go everywhere … except the toilet! So kill the king in the royal loo. In 1016 King Edmund Ironside made the mistake of going to the toilet…

1 While the King feasts, go to the toilet pit.

2 Lie down with your knife in your hand (never mind that you are lying in other people's poo).

3 When the King sits over the toilet pit strike upwards with your knife, through his bum into his bowels.

4 Escape. Have a bath. Have another bath.

King Ed, dead.

One report says the killer paid two servants to stick an iron hook into his bowels.

Slave trick

Nathaniel North (1680–1709) was a pirate. His best prizes weren't chests of gold – they were slaves. Now chasing and catching slaves is hard work. Nasty Nat found an easy way to do it. He went to the island of Madagascar. The Madagascans were fighting wars among themselves. The winners were left with lots of prisoners. Nat took the losers – it saved the winners having to feed them or kill them.

It worked well … until some Madagascans murdered him in his bed.

Top bodysnatching tip

If you had a dead body in the late 1700s you could sell it to doctors. They needed bodies to experiment on to find out how humans work. They were allowed to experiment on dead criminals, but not on ordinary people like you or me.

If you were a villain and you DIDN'T have a dead body then all you had to do was grab one from a grave. (Make sure it's a nice fresh one!) This was against the law … but it made you good money.

Here's a top tip from the best bodysnatchers…

1 Do NOT uncover the whole coffin. It's hard work and it takes time – you may get caught.

2 Uncover the top HALF of the coffin. Smash in the coffin lid.

3 Loop a rope under the corpse's arms and pull it out.

4 Stick it in a barrow and run to the doctor's.

> ### ❧ DID YOU KNOW…? ❧
>
> The highwayman villain Dick Turpin was hanged in York and buried in St George's churchyard in the city. He was dug up and buried in a doctor's garden till the doctor could start carving the corpse. But before he could, Turpin's friends dug the body up again and buried it in the churchyard a second time. This time they poured quicklime over the body to destroy it. Rest in pieces, Dick.

Top traitor tip

Benedict Arnold (1741–1801) was an American hero until he changed sides and became America's favourite villain. They trusted him. When they were at war with the British Ben switched sides to give American secrets to the British enemy. He then fought for his new Brit friends.

Ben had been wounded twice in the same leg at Quebec and Saratoga while he had been fighting for America against the Brits and so had to have a false leg fitted.

Rebel leader Thomas Jefferson was desperate to get his hands on Bad Ben to get some revenge. He said…

IF WE CATCH HIM WE'LL CUT OFF THAT AMERICAN LEG AND BURY IT WITH HONOUR … THE REST OF HIM WE'LL HANG!

They never did catch him and Bad Ben moved to England. He was never very popular with anyone, not even the Brits, and died in poverty … and so did his heroic American leg.

Money-making tip

Reverend Edward Free (1755–1843), a priest from Bedfordshire, made money by selling the lead from his church roof and the trees from the churchyard. He kept sheep in the church porch and cows and pigs roamed around the graves – even during a funeral.

Reverend Free whipped his helpers and ended up in a gun siege in the church. He finally fled to London where the wheel came off a coach and killed him.

BAP!

Escape trick

On 9 Jan 1838 a scary article appeared in *The Times* newspaper:

SPRING-HEELED JACK STRIKES

It seems that a gentlemen made a bet with one of his friends. He bet he would visit London houses in three disguises – a ghost, a bear and a devil.

He would enter gardens and frighten the people of the house. This villain has already driven seven ladies out of their senses.

This joker would usually pick on women and would tear at their clothes with claws before escaping. He had a trick of breathing blue flames from his mouth as he attacked. But Spring-heeled Jack's greatest trick was to escape by jumping over fences and walls using special boots that had springs in the heels.

Top con trick 1

In the 1840s the British government were always looking for new weapons to fight their wars. Samuel Alfred Warner (1794–1853) said he had an invisible shell. It didn't need gunpowder. He blew up two little ships to show how it worked … but no one was allowed to see how he did it.

Now YOU can see how he did it, can't you?

LOAD A BARREL OF GUNPOWDER ON TO A SHIP AT 1 P.M. AND LIGHT A 1-HOUR FUSE.

HAVE THE SHIP TOWED OUT FROM SHORE AND AT 2 P.M. HAVE EVERYONE WATCH IT.

TELL THEM YOU'VE FIRED YOUR INVISIBLE SHELL.

WATCH THE SHIP EXPLODE.

Then Warner asked for money to show the navy a 'long-range' shell – one that could wreck an enemy fort miles away. The government gave him £2,000.

But they didn't get what they expected! It was a hot-air balloon that carried an explosive over the target. It was supposed to land and go off.

It didn't. It missed … by miles. But the government went on believing him, and paying him, for 20 years.

The water bottle trick

Wild West bank robber Butch Cassidy (real name George Leroy Parker) was born in Utah in 1866 and was robbing trains before he was 20.

In 1889, Cassidy joined Tom McCarty. Inside the bank, McCarty held up a small bottle which he said contained high explosive.

IF I DROP THIS WE'LL ALL BE BLOWN INTO THE NEXT STATE!

* Nitro-glycerine

The bank gave him $21,000 to go away. As he left the bank with the cash, he threw the bottle into a waste-paper basket. It was full of water. Ho! Ho!

Top charmer's tip

George Joseph Smith (1872–1915) killed seven women by drowning them in their bath. First he would trick them into giving him all of their money and then he would say…

After they came back from the doctor Smith got them to take a bath. As they sat and soaked he placed a hand on their head and grabbed an ankle in the other hand. He pulled the ankle and pushed down on the head. The sudden rush of water into their lungs drowned them quickly. THEN George called the same doctor.

Then Smith changed his name, found another victim and so it went on. Until … the second woman's dad saw a report of the third victim. 'Hello,' he said, 'That's how MY daughter died! The police should be told!'

Savage Smith was arrested and hanged. His mistake was to try the same trick again and again.

At Smith's trial the police showed how to drown a woman in a bath! They used a nurse in a tub of water. It nearly killed her. And where did Smith's third bath victim die? In the city of … Bath!

Top con trick 2

Promise to make people rich. Sell them a brilliant idea. Get them to pay you … then disappear with the money and the secret.

Henry Ford made a fortune from his company – Ford motor cars. But still he wanted more money. One day he received a letter from a stranger.

22 April 1916
Farningdale, New York
Dear Mr Ford

The price of petrol is rising all the time. What if I told you I can make cars run on something cheaper – what if I told you I can make them run on water? Just add a little of my special mixture to a gallon of water and the car will run without petrol. Sell the special mix and you will make millions. All you have to do is pay me one million dollars. Pay me $100,000 now and the rest when you have sold the mix to the world. You have nothing to lose!
Your humble servant,

Professor Enricht.

Henry Ford saw a car run on a bucket of water … with a magic liquid added. He paid $10,000 for the secret. Enricht then sent the same letter to a gun-maker, Hiram Maxim.

Maxim said he'd give Enricht $100,000. Enricht sent back Henry Ford's money and took the Maxim money. He handed over an envelope and told Maxim not to open it till Enricht said he could.

Even the President of the US was thrilled to think the country would have so much cheap fuel.
Then Enricht disappeared.
Maxim opened the envelope.
It was full of blank paper.

POO BUMS

✶✶ DID YOU KNOW…? ✶✶

No one knows how Enricht made a car run on a bucket of water. But he may have found that a mixture of acetone and liquid acetylene will make a car run if it's added to water … for a while. But as Enricht could have told you…

A LITTLE BOTTLE OF MY MIXTURE COSTS FAR MORE THAN PETROL – AND AFTER FIFTY MILES IT WRECKS THE ENGINE. BUT WHAT DO I CARE? I'M £100,000 RICHER!

Crazed criminals

Villains are often not just bad, they're also mad... Bank robbers and burglars are small-time villains but in history there have been some criminals who brought misery to millions and crime to countless numbers. And some who have been mad with cruelty...

1 Robert De Belesme (1052–1130)

Rotten Robert was earl of Shropshire, Arundel and Shrewsbury – which is a bit greedy. He was a Norman baron at a time when England was pretty lawless. He had his captives lowered on to sharpened poles – impaled – rather than ask for a ransom. But even his family wasn't safe. One day his children were playing a game of hide and seek and hid behind his cloak. Robert went into a rage. It was said he tore out the eyes of his children. He had his wife locked in chains and thrown into a dungeon.

GRRRR

2 The Red Man (Middle Ages)

Some villains have no name. They are simply known by a nickname. The most famous of course is 'Jack the Ripper'.

But other nameless nasties have haunted our history. Take the case of the Red Man of Wales in the Middle Ages. If a newspaper had reported the case it might have looked like this:

VILLAGER VANQUISHES RED VILLAIN!

WOMAN IS WINNER IN BATTLE OF BLOOD

The people of Nanrhynan can sleep easy again. For a month they have been terrorized by a monstrous red-haired man. He stole chicken and lambs from their barns at night and was seen to eat them raw.

No one knows where the Red Man came from but he is said to be a Viking invader left behind when his comrades sailed away. He had the strength of ten and no man was able to defeat him … but a woman has!

Rhiannon Taff was left alone with her children in her cottage at the top of Nanrhynan valley and was warned about the monster muncher. But instead of locking herself away the Welsh wonder woman carefully left a kitchen window open – the sort of thing the Red Man loved.

Sure enough he reached her cottage and put one of his monstrous claws through the open window. But ruthless Rhiannon was ready! Ready with her awesome axe. With a single stroke she sliced through the hairy wrist and sent monster-man howling into the night.

In the morning light the villagers followed the trail of blood to a cave behind a waterfall. But there was no sign of the man.

Brave Rhiannon said, 'I'm going to pickle the hand and keep it to show my friends. Now if you'll excuse me I've a bit of blood to mop up from the kitchen floor!'

Her neighbour, Tegwyn Thomas, said, 'She's not a woman to mess with. She was braver than me, I have to hand it to her.'

3 Jacques Clement, France (1567–89)

King Henry III of France was vicious. He killed the Duke of Guise in 1588. How do you get rid of a dead duke? Cut your duke to pieces and have his body burnt. Finally, have the bones crushed to powder and have the ashes scattered to the wind.

But revenge was on the way. A monk called Jacques Clement asked to see Henry III and the guards let him in.

He WAS a harmless monk after all ... wasn't he? No, he was crazy.

As soon as Jacques was close enough he drew a knife and stabbed Henry to death.

The King's servants battered and hacked the monk to death.

☠ DID YOU KNOW...? ☠

The next King of France, Henry IV (1553–1610), was ALSO killed by a mad monk. Henry was riding in his carriage when it got stuck in a traffic jam. Mad monk François Ravaillac jumped on to the carriage wheel and thrust his dagger into the King's chest.

---

4 Ibrahim I 'The Mad' of Turkey (1616–48)

Ib was a jealous man. He heard that one of his 280 wives had another boyfriend. But he didn't know which wife. SO what did he do?

a) He started pulling out their fingernails, one at a time, till they told the truth.

b) He offered a million gold pieces to the wife who told him the truth.

c) He simply drowned them all.

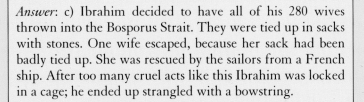

Answer: c) Ibrahim decided to have all of his 280 wives thrown into the Bosporus Strait. They were tied up in sacks with stones. One wife escaped, because her sack had been badly tied up. She was rescued by the sailors from a French ship. After too many cruel acts like this Ibrahim was locked in a cage; he ended up strangled with a bowstring.

5 Alexander Pearce, Australia (died 1823)

In the 1800s British criminals were sent to Australia as a punishment – 'transported'. (The Australians' revenge was to send us Kylie Minogue.)

Alexander Pearce was transported in 1819. He was a problem prisoner and by 1821 he'd had 150 lashes. So he decided to escape. His story is one of the most horrible in history…

Alexander Pearce was hanged. His body was cut up by doctors to experiment on.

His head was sent to the University of Pennsylvania's museum in the USA. It's still there.

Pearce killed his victims with an axe. It was sometimes slow and cruel. One victim, Mathers, was struck but still lived. He was given half an hour to say his prayers ... and then killed.

What did he pray? 'Give us this day our daily bread'?

6 Feargus O'Connor (1796–1855)

Some criminals are just plain daft. In 1840 an Irishman, Feargus O'Connor, decided to assassinate Queen Victoria ... but he didn't have a gun. He tried to make one out of a kettle, but it didn't work. Finally he got his hands on a very old pistol. He packed it with gunpowder ... but didn't have any bullets. Instead he packed it with tobacco! Feargus stepped out of a crowd and fired the pistol at the Queen as she drove past in her carriage.

This pointless action only gets him transported to Australia for 7 years. Durrrr ... why bother, Feargus?

COUGH!

✖ DID YOU KNOW? ✖

James Alexander (born 1700) was a cruel villain who was taken to court by a labourer who complained that James had piddled in his hat. The court let James off when he agreed to buy the victim a new (dry) hat. Mad as a hatter!

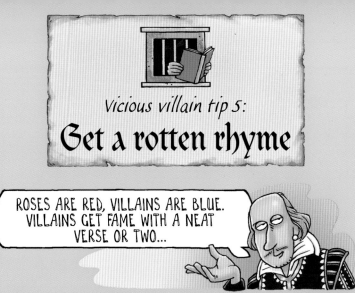

Vicious villain tip 5:
Get a rotten rhyme

ROSES ARE RED, VILLAINS ARE BLUE.
VILLAINS GET FAME WITH A NEAT
VERSE OR TWO...

Want to be remembered for your crimes? Get someone to write a poem about you. That's what these law-breaking lads and lasses did.

1 Robin Hood (around 1200)

Records show that a man with a name like Robin Hood lived in Wakefield, England. If you want to see where the 'Real' Robin Hood lived, go to Wakefield Bus Station – his house was somewhere underneath the bus stop … maybe.

The story says Robin fought for his king, Edward II. When the King was thrown off the throne Rob had to hide in Barnsdale Forest. Lots of stories were told about this outlaw. But his death is a real warning that says 'Trust nobody'.

Robin grew old and sickly from all that living in the forest and turned to a relation for help, his cousin Elizabeth de Staynton, who was a naughty nun.

The tales of Robin Hood were told at first as poems. They are old English and hard to follow. Here's a new version…

Robin grew quite old and grey,
Long past robbing rich (they say).
He said, 'I don't feel very good ...
It's all that living in the wood ...
... Bad for a wrinklie like me!

'To Kirklees Abbey I'll be buzzin'
The prioress there she's my cousin.
My cousin Beth is the top nun
She'll feed me up with cakes and buns ...
... And maybe a nice cup of tea.'

Now Robin had an ene-mee
Called Roger of old Donkes-lee.
Rob doesn't know the man he hates
With good old Beth was best of mates ...
... and she fancied him too.

So Rob arrived and Prioress said,
'Just lie down, Rob, upon this bed.
The problem is, dear Robin Hood,
You're full of too much real bad blood ...
... so we'll let some out.'

But that bad nun she played a trick,
She took a knife and made a nick.
He thought he'd lose a little blood
Instead she let out quite a flood ...
... and finished him off.

And so he died in pools of red
And all the poor men wept (it's said).
So don't go trusting nuns called Beth
Or they may bring about your death ...
... or worse.

🎮 **DID YOU KNOW...?** 🎮
Robin's favourite Merry Man was Little John. But not many people know Little John used to work for Rob's enemy the Sheriff of Nottingham. Then one day a servant was slow to serve Little John – John went off in a huff and joined Robin's gang. When Robin was murdered by Elizabeth it was Little John who buried him.

2 Alice Holt (1600s)

Alice Holt poisoned her mother with arsenic and a poem of the time told the tale...

> *A dreadful case of poison, such as we seldom hear,*
> *Committed was at Stockport, in the county of Cheshire.*
> *Where a mother named Mary Bailey, they did so cruelly slaughter,*
> *By poison administer all in her beer, by her own daughter.*
> *She made a plan to murder her, as we now see so clear,*
> *To put a quantity of arsenic into her poor mother's beer.*
> *But there's no doubt the base wretch did her poor mother slay,*
> *For which on Chester scaffold her life did forfeit pay.*
> *So all young women a warning take, by this poor wretch you see,*
> *A-hanging for her mother's sake on Chester's fatal tree.*

What a crime ... against poetry!

3 Eugene Aram (1704–59)

Eugene was a thief, a murderer ... and a schoolteacher!

He lived in Knaresborough, Yorkshire, and in 1745 robbed and murdered a shoemaker.

Fourteen years later a skeleton was found in a cave and everyone thought it was the dead shoemaker ... it wasn't! But teacher Eugene was arrested and hanged.

His body was hanged in chains near Knaresborough and left to rot. As the bones dropped out of the cage Eugene's wife picked them up to bury them.

When the head fell out it was sent to a museum in London ... and it's still there today.

Eugene would be just another forgotten murderer but his tale was turned into a very popular – but really awful – poem. Want to impress your teacher? Recite a couple of vile verses...

One that had never done me wrong,
A feeble man and old:
I led him to a lonely field;
The moon shone clear and cold:
Now here, said I, this man shall die,
And I will have his gold!

Two sudden blows with a ragged stick,
And one with a heavy stone,
One hurried gash with a hasty knife,
And then the deed was done;
There was nothing lying at my foot
But lifeless flesh and bone!

With breathless speed, like a soul in chase,
I took him up and ran;
There was no time to dig a grave
Before the day began:
In a lonesome wood, with heaps of leaves,
I hid the murder'd man.

4 William Burke (1792–1829) and William Hare (1790–1859)

Burke and Hare made a good living selling corpses in Edinburgh. But their crimes were remembered even in children's rhymes…

Burke's the butcher,
Hare's the thief,
Knox the boy that buys
the beef!

Doctors like Dr Knox paid Burke and Hare £8 to £14 for a fresh corpse. The doctor didn't ask where the bodies came from. In fact, Burke and Hare were murdering their lodging-house guests. They caught the victim asleep and slapped a tar cloth over their nose and mouth till they snuffed it.

The pair were caught. The police made a deal with Hare…

TELL US THE TRUTH AND WE'LL HANG BURKE AND SET YOU FREE.

IT'S A DEAL!

Hare ratted on his partner who was hanged. He changed his name and went off to live in Carlisle, England.

Someone recognized Hare and a mob attacked him. They threw lime in his face to blind him. He died penniless in 1859. Don't trust your partner in crime.

5 Mary Ann Cotton (1830–73)

Misery Mary of County Durham in England killed about 15 of her own children and three husbands. She fed the children with arsenic poison from a teapot.

They died a slow and painful death.

She tried to have her last child taken into a workhouse but the workhouse refused to take the boy. Mary said…

NEVER MIND … HE WON'T GROW UP

I'M AS FIT AS A FLEA!

WHAT? HE LOOKS A HEALTHY LAD TO ME!

A week later the boy was dead. Mary was arrested and hanged. A hundred years later Durham children still sang this skipping song:

Mary Ann Cotton, she's dead and she's rotten,
She lies on her bed with her eyes wide open.
Sing, sing! What shall I sing?
Mary Ann Cotton is tied up with string.
Where, where? Up in the air,
Selling black puddings a penny a pair.

Black puddings? Swollen tubes of blood … like the legs of a hanged woman. Nasty song for a nasty woman.

6 Amelia Dyer (died 1896)

In Victorian times unwanted babies were sent to a 'baby farmer'. You gave this woman five or ten pounds and she cared for the baby till she found it a new home ... sometimes.

Amelia Dyer just took the money and killed the kid.

In 1895 she moved to Reading, and put an advert in the paper to say she would look after children. In March that year a bargeman pulled the corpse of a baby out of the Thames.

It was wrapped in a parcel – but the paper had been used to send a parcel to Mrs. Dyer so her name and address was on it! It didn't take Sherlock Holmes to track her down. But by the time Mrs Dyer was arrested six more of the little corpses had been found.

She was hanged in June 1896. No one will ever know how many she murdered, but at the time of her arrest she had been baby-farming for fifteen years.

Like many wicked women she had a song written about her execution and the way she would roast in Hell...

Sing along ...

The Old Baby Farmer

The old baby farmer has been executed
It's about time she was put out of the way
She was a bad woman it is not disputed
Not a word in her favour can anyone say

> That old baby farmer, that wretched Mrs Dyer
> At the Old Bailey her wages be paid
> In times long ago we have made a big fire
> And roasted so nicely that wicked old Jade
>
> Down through the trapdoor she's quickly disappearing
> Her poor little victims in front of her eyes
> The sound of her own death bell she'll be a-hearing
> The rope round her neck … how quickly time flies

7 Lizzie on the loose (1860–1927)

Lizzie Borden was America's most famous killer of the 1800s. When Lizzie was 32 years old she was accused of hacking her father and stepmother to death with an axe.

All the evidence pointed to her – yet she was found not guilty and set free. Her story has been turned into a ballet, a film and a musical. But most famous is the kids' song!

Lizzie Borden took an axe,
Gave her mother forty whacks;
When she saw what she had done
She gave her father forty-one!

YOU'RE SICK

8 Bonnie Parker (1910–34)

Bonnie Parker and her partner Clyde Barrow robbed banks. They also murdered 12 people who got in their way.

Bonnie knew it couldn't last so she wrote her own funeral poem. It went:

> *Some day they will go down together*
> *And they will bury them side by side.*
> *To a few it means grief,*
> *To the law it's relief,*
> *But it's death to Bonnie and Clyde.*

Soon after she wrote it the pair were gunned down. But they did not 'bury them side by side'.

Two lonely ghosts.

Evil ends

I did warn you that the bad news is some villains have come to very nasty ends. So, when you become a villain, how would YOU like to die? Here's your choice, from deadly thrones to barrels of wine...

1 Sigurd 1 of Orkney (died AD 892)

Viking Sigurd was a cheat! He conquered and ruled Orkney well, but then he attacked Scotland and made enemies.

He told his chief enemy Maelbrigte…

LET'S SETTLE THIS ONCE AND FOR ALL. I WILL FIGHT YOU TO THE DEATH WITH 40 HORSEMEN

I AGREE

Sigurd turned up with 40 horses … but with two men on each horse[6]. The Vikings won, of course. Sigurd lopped off the head of Maelbrigte, fastened it on his saddle and rode home. But Maelbrigte had buck teeth. One of the teeth rubbed against Sigurd's leg. It made a wound which turned septic and Sigurd died of the blood poisoning.

That's the tooth, the whole tooth and nothing but the tooth.

6 For those of you still at Key Stage 0 for maths (as I am) that's 80 Viking men against 40 Scots. Those of you with Key Stage 1 maths will know that the Vikings outnumbered the Scots two to one.

2 High Prince Almos of Hungary (died AD 896)

This powerful prince rampaged around Europe and beat lots of people in battles. But he was told…

> YOU WILL BE FIRST OF A LONG LINE OF GREAT KINGS … BUT NEVER ENTER THE LAND OF PANNONIA

> GOLLY

The Pecheneg people there had a habit of turning enemy skulls into drinking cups. That gives us a bit of a clue why it would be wise to keep out of their lands in Pannonia.

So Almos went to Pannonia … these villains never learn, do they? He was defeated and sacrificed by horse. Here's how…

fig I First take four horses and four ropes.

fig II. Tie one end of each rope to each horse and the other ends to the wrist or ankle of the villain.

fig III Frighten the horses so they all run off in different directions

fig IV Pick up the bits and put them on show.

What have you got? Five bleeding villain bits.

3 Bela of Hungary (died 1063)

Bela went to war with his brother Andras. As Andras tried to run away he was killed. Bela snatched the crown of Hungary. But he made enemies. He sat down on the high throne of Hungary under a fine canopy.

Splat! The canopy collapsed and killed Bela. Some artful assassin had sawn through the posts that held it up.

4 The Duke of Clarence (died 1478)

Cruel Clarence wanted the throne of England ... but his brother Richard stood in the way. Clarence plotted against Richard and rotten Rich found out.

It is said that Richard had Clarence drowned in a barrel of wine. Some people say Richard politely asked Clarence to choose...

SO HOW WOULD YOU LIKE TO DIE, BRUV?

ER ... OLD AGE?

MALMSEY WINE

Others say the drowning is just a story. A body was dug up many years later that was probably Clarence's. It had been beheaded. A noble way to die … so wine not?

5 Pedro de Valdivia (c. 1500–54)

The Spanish Conquistadors smashed the natives of Peru to steal their gold. Pedro was captured and the Peruvian warriors gave him a pot of gold … scalding, melted gold.

They poured it down his throat and said (in Inca language)…

> YOU WERE THIRSTY FOR OUR GOLD, SO DRINK!

Of course that story is a bit too clever to believe. Other reports say Pedro de Valdivia…
- was beaten to death
- was pierced with a wooden stake
- had his heart cut out and eaten.

6 Henry II of France (1519–59)

Hen was Catholic and he hated Protestants like his neighbours in Austria. He attacked them and burned them alive. If they spoke Protestant prayers their tongues were cut out. Even if he just thought you were a Protestant you'd be imprisoned for life.

Henry enjoyed jousting as a knight … you know, charging at one another with lances.

But Henry was KING … so he couldn't have a plain iron helmet, oh no. He had to have one with a golden visor to shield his face. But gold is soft (like Henry's brain).

> HE CAN HAVE MY PROTESTANT BRAIN IN A MINUTE

A rival's lance splintered and smashed through the soft golden visor. The splinter went into Henry's eye and popped out of his ear. He took ten days to die, slowly and horribly.

7 Jerry Abershaw (1773–95)

Being a villain is no fun if you can't have a joke … even in the bad times.

Highwayman Jerry Abershaw was sentenced to death for his crimes. He enjoyed the last couple of weeks of his life…

• When a judge sentenced a villain he would put on a black cap and speak these deadly words…

> *The sentence of the court upon you is, that you be taken from this place to a lawful prison and thence to a place of execution and that you be hanged by the neck until you are dead; and that your body be afterwards buried within the grounds of the prison. And may the Lord have mercy on your soul. Amen.*

To show he didn't care, Jerry ALSO put on a black cap as the judge sentenced him. He replied…

> *And YOU are a murderer.*

• While Jerry waited for his execution someone sent him a bowl of cherries. He used the cherry juice to paint pictures of his crimes on the prison-cell walls.

- When he was taken to hang outside the prison walls he wore an open white shirt and a flower in his mouth. He joked with the crowd who'd come to see him die.
- The last thing he did was take off his boots!

> MY MUM ALWAYS SAID I WAS SUCH A CRIMINAL I'D DIE WITH MY BOOTS ON ... WELL YOU WERE WRONG, MA!!!

Good people (like you and me) are supposed to die peacefully in bed – with our boots OFF.

8 Constantine Hangerli, Prince of Wallachia (died 1799)

Con was a terror to the peasants. If they didn't pay their taxes they were killed.

He was not top of the peasant pops.

In 1799 he lost a lot of battles and his boss, Sultan Selim III, was not pleased. He sent an assassin to kill Con. The assassin…
- strangled him
- shot him twice in the chest
- stabbed him
- beheaded him

9 Dan Morgan (1830–65)

This Australian outlaw was also known as John Smith, Sydney Bill, Dan Owen, Down-the-River Jack and Bill the Native. He attacked people on the road, beat them half to death … then sobbed, 'Forgive me! I'm sorry!' So that's all right then.

At Peechelba he went into a tavern and held all the people hostage. But one serving girl slipped out and warned the police. When Morgan came out with his hostages he was shot in the back and died six hours later.

His body was taken to Wangaratta, where a strange thing happened. The body was propped up in a stable and shown to the public. His eyes were opened and one of his pistols was put in his hand. Photographs were then taken. Lumps of his hair were then chopped from the head as souvenirs.

The police stopped it, but worse was to come. Morgan's head was cut off and sent to Melbourne; his headless body was buried at the Wangaratta cemetery.

10 Grigori Rasputin (1869–1916)

The Mad Monk Rasputin became a great friend of the Russian royal family. He used his power to get lots of gifts and even chatted up the Queen and her daughter.

The Russian nobles hated him and Prince Felix Yusupov plotted to kill him. Felix SAID…

BUT … every time Felix told the story he changed it. The TRUTH may be different. The body of the monk had NO poison and he HADN'T drowned. He died from a bullet in the head.

Epilogue

Villains come in all shapes and sizes, from school bullies who will knock out your teeth for a bag of sweets, to 'great leaders' whose orders lead to misery for millions. Now you have some idea about how some villains became villains. But would you want to copy them? If YOU fancy a bit of murder and mayhem just remember, it's not all fun and games.

SOME villains can end up happy ever after. Captain Henry Morgan (1635–88) was a Welsh sea captain who became a pirate. After years of robbery he settled down. He was made 'Sir' Henry by King Charles II and sent to govern Jamaica. Happy ending… Of course he died horribly from drinking too much rum, but there are lots of worse ways to go…

I'LL DRINK TO THAT!

Most villains bring misery, suffering and death to the world … then end up end up miserable, suffering and dead.

Villains have been …

Villainy is fun when you're winning ... but you end up making so many enemies they get you in the end.

IS IT WORTH IT?

Interesting Index

Hang on! This isn't one of your boring old indexes. This is a horrible index. It's the only index in the world where you will find 'fried prisoners', 'cosy coffins', 'guts in gold bowls' and all the other things you really HAVE to know if you want to be a horrible historian. Read it and creep.

Caesar, Julius (Austrian villain)
10–11
cannibals 67
Capone, Al (American gangster) 29
Cassidy, Butch (American outlaw)
27, 59
cats, tormenting 35
ceilings, hanging from 34
Charles II, King of England 44–5, 86
Clarence, Richard Duke of
(English villain) 81–2
Clement, Jacques (French
assassin/monk) 65
Cleopatra VII (Egyptian queen)
46–7
coffins
    cosy 13
    nailing down lids of 11
    smashing lids of 55
Columbus, Christopher
(Portuguese explorer) 42–3
corpses
    carving up 56
    digging up 17
    selling 74
    stuffed with straw 18
Cotton, Mary Ann (English
murderer) 75
Crown Jewels 44–5

Dillinger, John (American
gangster) 29, 38–9
dogs
    dead 8–9
    hunting 52
    throwing off roof 10

tormenting 35
torn apart by 16
Domitian (Roman emperor) 30
Dózsa, György (Hungarian rebel)
34–5
Dudley, Richard (English
highwayman) 12–13
Dyer, Amelia (English baby
farmer) 76–7

**Edmund Ironside, King of
England** 54
Elagabalus (Roman emperor/sun
god) 7–8
Enricht, Professor (American
trickster) 61–2
Eustace (French monk/pirate) 20–2
eyes, torn out 63

Fawkes, Guy (gunpowder plotter)
38
Flower, Margaret (English witch)
49–50
Ford, Henry (American car
manufacturer) 61–2

Genghis Khan (Mongol warrior)
17
Godwin (earl of Wessex) 31–2
grown-ups, grumpy 5
guts, in gold bowls 8–9

Hall, Ben (Australian outlaw) 26–7
Hangerli, Constantine (Prince of
Wallachia) 84

Don't miss these horribly handy handbooks for all the gore and more!

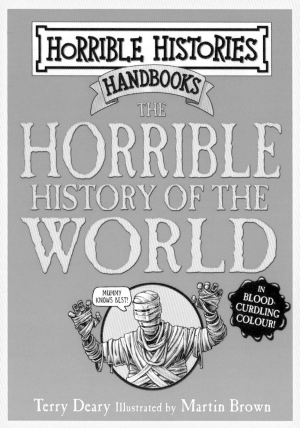

ISBN: 978 1407 10350 1 £5.99

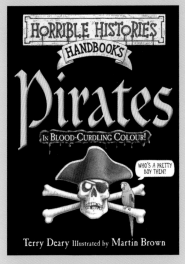

ISBN: 978 0439 95578 2 £5.99

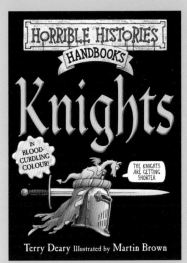

ISBN: 978 0439 95577 5 £5.99

ISBN: 978 0439 94986 6 £5.99

ISBN: 978 0439 94330 7 £5.99

Make sure you've got the whole horrible lot!

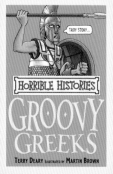

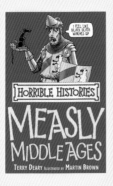

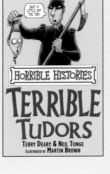

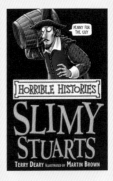

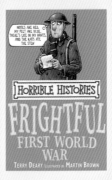

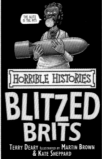

Terry Deary was born at a very early age, so long ago he can't remember. But his mother, who was there at the time, says he was born in Sunderland, north-east England, in 1946 – so it's not true that he writes all *Horrible Histories* from memory. At school he was a horrible child only interested in playing football and giving teachers a hard time. His history lessons were so boring and so badly taught, that he learned to loathe the subject. *Horrible Histories* is his revenge.

Martin Brown was born in Melbourne, on the proper side of the world. Ever since he can remember he's been drawing. His dad used to bring back huge sheets of paper from work and Martin would fill them with doodles and little figures. Then, quite suddenly, with food and water, he grew up, moved to the UK and found work doing what he's always wanted to do: drawing doodles and little figures.